Juices for Runners

Juicer Recipes, Diet and Nutrition Plan to Support Optimal Health, Weight loss and Peformance Whilst Running and Jogging (Food for Fitness Series)

Lars Andersen

Published by Nordic Standard Publishing

Atlanta, Georgia USA

ISBN 978-1-484145-10-4

All Rights Reserved

No part of this book may be reproduced or transmitted for resale or use by any party other than the individual purchaser who is the sole authorized user of this information. Purchaser is authorized to use any of the information in this publication for his or her own use only. All other reproduction or transmission, or any form or by any means, electronic or mechanical, including photocopying, recording or by any informational storage or retrieval system, is prohibited without express written permission from the author.

Lars Andersen

Copyright © 2012 Lars Andersen

What Our Readers Are Saying

"I never realized that sports nutrition could be so tasty -- and affordable!"

★★★★☆ **Mary R. Rodriguez (Laredo, TX)**

"The second book I've bought by Lars Andersen, highly recommended!"

★★★★★ **Katie F. Knox (Duncan, NE)**

"This book has it all. It's definitely helped take my training up a gear"

★★★★★ **Bill M. Keller (Joes, CO)**

Exclusive Bonus Download: Sprints And Marathons

Sure-fire Ways To Master Your Running Efforts!

This Book Is One Of The Most Valuable Resources In The World When It Comes To Getting Serious Results In Your Life!

Running is the act by which animals, including human beings, move by the power of the feet. Speeds may vary and range from jogging to a sprint. A lot of individuals compete in track events that place participants in a contest to test speed in a sprint or endurance in a marathon. The running mechanics are the same, but additional factors are very different in a marathon versus a sprint.

Consider this...

Whether your goal is to determine a fresh personal record in your next 5k, win your age bracket at the following charity run or qualify for a state or national contest, you may learn to run faster.

Are you ready?

Introducing… Sprints And Marathons

This powerful tool will provide you with everything you need to know to be a success and achieve your goal.

Who Can Use This Book?

- Life Coaches
- Runners
- Personal Development Enthusiasts
- Self Improvement Bloggers
- Business owners
- Internet marketers
- Network marketers
- Web Publishers
- Writers and Content Creators
- And Many More!

<u>Go to the end of this book for the download link for this Bonus!</u>

Thank you for downloading my book. Please REVIEW this book on Amazon. I need your feedback to make the next edition better. Thank you so much!

Books by Lars Andersen

<u>The Smoothies for Runners Book</u>

Juices for Runners

Smoothies for Cyclists

Juices for Cyclists

Paleo Diet for Cyclists

Smoothies for Triathletes

Juices for Triathletes

Paleo Diet for Triathletes

Smoothies for Strength

Juices for Strength

Paleo Diet for Strength

Paleo Diet Smoothies for Strength

Smoothies for Golfers

Juices for Golfers

Table of Contents

JUICING AND JUICES FOR RUNNERS **8**

FUELLING YOUR RUN **9**

    CARBOHYDRATES 9

    FATS 11

    PROTEIN 11

JUICING UP! **12**

FLUIDS AND HYDRATION **15**

JUICES WITH A TWIST **17**

GETTING THE MOST FROM A JUICE **19**

GENERAL INFORMATION ABOUT YOUR JUICES **21**

PRE-RUN JUICES **22**

    1. STRAWBERRY AND MINT JUICE 23

    2. PAPAYA AND LEMON JUICE 24

    3. BANANA, APPLE AND CINNAMON JUICE 25

    4. PINEAPPLE AND PEAR JUICE 26

    5. WATERMELON, MELON AND PEAR JUICE WITH SPINACH 27

    6. KIWI, PEAR AND STRAWBERRY JUICE 27

    7. CARROT, ORANGE AND PINEAPPLE JUICE 28

    8. CUCUMBER, KIWI AND PEAR JUICE WITH MINT 29

    9. POMEGRANATE AND BLUEBERRIES JUICE 30

    10. APPLE AND PLUMS JUICE 30

    11. PINEAPPLE AND PEACH JUICE 31

    12. ROMAINE LETTUCE, APPLE AND MELON JUICE 31

    13. CUCUMBER AND POMEGRANATE JUICE 32

PRE-RUN JUICES - FOR RUNS LASTING 4 OR MORE HOURS **33**

    14. ORANGE AND APRICOT JUICE 34

    15. COCONUT, AND GUAVA JUICE WITH LEMON AND MINT 35

    16. PASSION FRUIT AND RASPBERRIES JUICE 36

    17. CHERRY JUICE 36

    18. KIWI AND PLUM JUICE 37

    19. MANGO AND PEAR JUICE 38

    20. PINEAPPLE, BANANA AND BROCCOLI JUICE 39

    21. MELON, KIWI, PEAR AND WATERCRESS JUICE WITH MINT 40

    22. PAPAYA AND PRUNES JUICE 41

    23. BLACKBERRIES, RAISINS AND BEET JUICE 42

POST-RUN JUICES **43**

24. RASPBERRY AND LEMON JUICE 43
25. BANANA AND BLACKBERRIES JUICE 44
26. COCONUT, PAPAYA, GUAVA JUICE 44
27. CURRANTS AND LEMON JUICE 45
28. GUAVA AND CHERRY JUICE 45
29. BEETROOT, BLACKBERRY AND STRAWBERRY JUICE 46
30. PASSION, FRUIT AND LEMON JUICE 47
31. CUCUMBER, WATERMELON AND CHERRY JUICE 47
32. LOQUAT, PEACH AND APRICOT JUICE 48
33. CURRANT AND BLACKBERRY JUICE 49
34. PUMPKIN, ORANGE AND LEMON JUICE 50
35. APRICOT AND GUAVA JUICE WITH KALE 51

EXCLUSIVE BONUS DOWNLOAD: SPRINTS AND MARATHONS.. 52

ONE LAST THING... 54

Disclaimer

While all attempts have been made to provide effective, verifiable information in this Book, neither the Author nor Publisher assumes any responsibility for errors, inaccuracies, or omissions. Any slights of people or organizations are unintentional.

This Book is not a source of medical information, and it should not be regarded as such. This publication is designed to provide accurate and authoritative information in regard to the subject matter covered. It is sold with the understanding that the publisher is not engaged in rendering a medical service. As with any medical advice, the reader is strongly encouraged to seek professional medical advice before taking action.

Juicing and Juices for Runners

"Running is the greatest metaphor for life, because you get out of it what you put into it" - Oprah Winfrey

Juicing is a fast and efficient way to maximize your nutrient intake. A fresh juice every morning before a run is a great way to energize your body without overloading your stomach with heavy foods that might lead to discomfort as you exercise.

The nutrients contained in juiced fruits and vegetables are readily absorbed by your body as the insoluble fiber that slows digestion is removed in the juicing process. In this "pre-digested" form, the health-boosting vitamin and mineral content is effectively "unlocked" and can therefore be of maximum benefit to your body.

Fruits and vegetables provide energy to fuel your run and they are also packed with vitamins, minerals and antioxidants which help to give your immune system a boost. Many varieties also contain anti-inflammatory properties which aid your body's recovery process after a hard or prolonged effort. Just as a car engine needs quality fuel to perform at its best, your body also needs quality fuel to give a quality performance. A delicious, nutritious juice is a convenient way to provide premium fuel for your body.

Fuelling Your Run

The key to getting the most from a juice is to use a juicing machine that allows the maximum nutrition to be extracted from the fruits and vegetables you choose. A quality juicer not only extracts the juice from the flesh but also from the peelings, seeds and pits. Not all juicers are suitable for all fruits - citrus fruits require a citrus juicer for example - so it's important to consider the type of produce you want to juice to ensure you get the best machine for your needs. Machines which limit the amount of heat generated in the juicing process also help to maximize the nutritional content by preserving the live enzyme content and antioxidant benefits. Raw fruit and vegetable juices contain enzymes that help your body to convert food into energy. All of your body's metabolic processes, including the conversion of foods into fuel, generate the formation of free radicals. These are chemicals which can be harmful to your health if left unchecked. Antioxidants protect your body against free radicals and they are abundant in a huge variety of fruits and vegetables. This makes a fresh juice a great pre-run source of health-boosting energy and also a post-run source of vital nutrients to help your body recover, regenerate and refuel in preparation for your next run.

The longer the duration or the greater the intensity of your runs, the more energy your body needs to keep going. The foods you eat are your body's only source of energy-providing calories so eating a balanced mix of quality foods is the only way to provide your body with the quality fuel it needs to give a quality performance. A balanced diet contains a healthy mix of carbohydrates, fats, protein, vitamins and minerals.

Carbohydrates

Carbohydrates are described as "the athlete's best friend" as they provide the main source of energy to fuel performance. They can be split into two categories:

Simple carbohydrates - sources include:

Sugary foodstuffs such as candy, cakes and sodas

Honey, in the form of glucose

Fruits and vegetables, in the form fructose and sucrose

Milk and dairy products, in the form of lactose

Malted wheat and barley, sprouting grains and malt extract, in the form of maltose

Molasses, dextrose, corn syrup and invert syrup.

Simple carbohydrates or **sugars** provide a fast-acting, virtually "instant" source of energy.

Complex carbohydrates - sources include:

Starchy foods such as bread and potatoes

Cereals

Pasta

Complex carbohydrates or **starch** provide a relatively slow-acting, steady source of energy. **Fiber** is also a complex carbohydrate, providing a steady source of energy with the added benefit of promoting regular, healthy bowel movements. The fiber content of fruits and vegetables helps to slow the energy release from the natural sugars, thereby helping to keep you healthfully energized for longer. Fiber can be further categorized as insoluble or soluble. Insoluble fiber is found in the skins of many fruits and vegetables, therefore the juicing process removes this form in most cases. Soluble fiber is found in the flesh of a variety of fruits and in some vegetables, therefore it remains present in most juices. Juicing fruits and vegetables gives your body a break from the process of digesting insoluble fiber. With the fiber removed, only water, vitamins and minerals remain, allowing for a much faster uptake of nutrients.

All forms of carbohydrate are broken down into glucose and glycogen before they can be used. Complex carbohydrates are broken down more slowly than simple carbohydrates, resulting in a slower release of energy, but honey is the only simple carbohydrate that can be used by your body straight away. Glucose and glycogen are your body's source of fuel as you run and they are inter-convertible. When you have a sufficient supply of glucose, your body stores any excess carbohydrates in the form of glycogen in your liver and muscles. If the supply of glucose then falls short of the energy demand, your body converts the stored glycogen into glucose ready for use.

One gram of carbohydrate provides four calories. However, your body can only store a limited amount of glycogen, with the muscles able to store enough for up to around two hours of intense exercise. After exercising, your body's ability to store glycogen is elevated. This period of around 30 minutes is known as the "glycogen window" and consuming appropriate foods in this window helps replenish glycogen stores, promote muscle repair and restoration, and thereby aid recovery after a long or intense run.

Fats

Fats also provide energy with one gram of fat providing nine calories. They act as a carrier for fat-soluble vitamins, including vitamins A, D, K, and E, they provide insulation for your body, and they protect vital organs. Many runners avoid fat in their diet, believing it to be unhealthy, but not all fats are equal and "healthy" fat is an essential element of a balanced diet.

Healthy fats:

Monounsaturated fatty acids - sources include olive oil, rapeseed oil, avocados, nuts and seeds.

Polyunsaturated fatty acids - sources include most vegetable oils, fish oils and oily fish. These also contain the essential fatty acids **omega-6** and **omega-3**. Good sources of omega-6 include olive oil and sunflower oil. Good sources of omega-3 include soya bean oil, rapeseed oil, walnuts, linseed or flax seeds and oil fish such as sardines, salmon and mackerel.

The average Western individual has around 60 times more energy stored in their body as fat than energy stored as glycogen in the liver and muscles. During endurance sports such as long-distance running, the body conserves as much of its glycogen reserves as possible by using some of its fat stores for energy. However, compared to carbohydrate, fat is a very slow source of energy, meaning that as the intensity of the exercise increases, the body switches to using glycogen to provide a faster release of energy. One potential bonus of fat consumption for runners is that it provides over twice the calories of carbohydrate, weight for weight, without creating too much bulk in the stomach.

Protein

Protein is essentially the body's muscle-builder but it is only used as a source of energy if your body's glycogen stores have been depleted. However, protein is of particular value to runners as it plays an important role in repairing the muscles that may suffer damage through repetitive wear and tear.

Juicing Up!

Fruits and vegetables contain carbohydrates, making them a nutritious way to top up your glycogen stores before a run and to replenish your stores after a run. They are also a rich source of vitamins, minerals and antioxidants, making them extremely important in terms of promoting and maintaining optimum health. The plant proteins contained in vegetables help to promote healthy tissue growth and repair, making them of particular benefit after long or intense runs that may lead to muscle damage.

The benefits of running on fruit juice:

Any combination of juiced fruits will provide energy-giving carbohydrates so your choice is a matter of personal taste. The antioxidant properties of many fruits can also help to reduce the effects of muscular damage generated through training. Vitamin C, vitamin E and beta-carotene are particularly effective at limiting the potentially damaging effects of free radicals. Popular choices include:

Grapefruit - a rich source of vitamin C and a good source of pectin which provides fiber.

Apples - a good source of vitamin C, bioflavonoids and soluble fiber. Bioflavonoids are powerful antioxidants.

Pears - a good source of vitamin C, potassium, bioflavonoids and pectin. Potassium is essential for the transmission of all nerve impulses.

Kiwi fruit - a rich source of vitamin C and a good source of potassium.

Cherries - a good source of potassium and a useful source of vitamin C. On-going research has found that cherry juice contains anti-inflammatory properties which may be of additional benefit to runners. A study involving marathon runners concluded that those who drank cherry juice recovered faster after training than those who did not. The antioxidant content helps to reduce inflammation, thereby helping to promote faster muscle recovery.

Apricots - a rich source of beta-carotene, the plant form of vitamin A which helps to protect against free radicals, and vitamin C.

Watermelon - contains vitamin C and potassium which works in tandem with sodium to help regulate the body's fluid balance.

Blueberries - contain as much as five times more antioxidant properties than other fruits! When blueberries are out of season, frozen varieties provide a useful alternative, or cranberries, grapes, blackberries and goji berries all make good substitutes.

As a general guide, fruits with orange or dark yellow flesh provide a good source of beta-carotene, and fruits with red flesh offer a good source of lycopene. The combination of beta-carotene and lycopene is thought to be very effective in terms of protecting your body against free radicals.

Fruits with a low water content often blend better than juice. Adding blended fruits to a juice, or putting back some of the pulp created in the juicing process, is a tasty way to thicken the consistency of a juice and increase the fiber content if desired. Fruits suitable for blending include:

Strawberries- a rich source of vitamin C and also an aid to the absorption of iron from vegetables. Iron is essential for the production of hemoglobin, the oxygen carrying pigment found in red blood cells.

Bananas - a rich source of potassium.

Avocados - a rich source of vitamin E and a good source of potassium. Avocados also have a high "healthy" fat content and can contain as many as 400 calories per fruit!

The benefits of running on vegetable juice:

Vegetables also offer a healthful source of carbohydrates for energy and many vegetables contain health boosting vitamin, mineral and antioxidant properties along with plant protein. Popular choices include:

Carrot - a rich source of beta-carotene.

Beets - a rich source of nutrients, including folate, an essential vitamin for cell health, potassium and vitamin C. The leafy tops contain beta-carotene, calcium and iron. Research has also found that drinking juiced beets on a regular basis can enhance a runner's tolerance to high-intensity exercise.

Celery - a good source of potassium.

Romaine Lettuce - a useful source of folate and beta-carotene

Cauliflower - a good source of vitamin C.

Cabbage - a rich source of vitamin C, vitamin K, and a good source of vitamin E, potassium and beta-carotene. Vitamin K is essential in the formation of many proteins.

Broccoli - another rich source of vitamin C. Broccoli also contains beta-carotene, iron and potassium, and is high in bioflavonoids and other antioxidants.

Pumpkin - a good source of beta-carotene and vitamin E. Pumpkin seeds are rich in iron, phosphorus, potassium, magnesium and zinc. Pumpkin juice is a favorite among Harry Potter fans!

Spinach - a rich source of carotenoids, including beta-carotene and lutein, which are powerful antioxidants. Also contains vitamin C and potassium.

Collard Greens - a good source of omega-3 essential fatty acids which have anti-inflammatory properties.

Kale - a good source of iron, calcium, vitamin C and beta-carotene.

Fennel - contains beta-carotene and folate, but particularly useful for adding flavor.

Watercress - contains vitamin C, beta-carotene and iron, and is also 91 percent water.

Green fruits and vegetables contain chlorophyll which has been shown to stimulate the production of hemoglobin, the oxygen carrying pigment in red blood cells. This can lead to improvements in your oxygen uptake and your body's ability to utilize it, referred to as your VO2 max, as well as giving your overall energy levels a boost. This is great news for competitive distance runners as improvements in VO2 max can lead to significant improvements in race times. A nutritious green juice can be made with green leafy vegetables; cruciferous vegetables, including broccoli, cauliflower and cabbage; grasses, including wheat grass and barley grass; algae, including chlorella and spirulina (also available in powder form); vegetable sprouts and sea vegetables. Most green vegetables are naturally alkaline which provides an additional benefit to runners. One cause of running fatigue is the elevation of acidity levels in your blood. Regularly consuming green vegetables helps to regulate the acidity of your blood and thereby improve your running performance by allowing you to train for longer without fatigue. A green juice is an extremely efficient way to "get your greens" on a daily basis!

A juice containing a flavorsome mix of fruits and vegetables consumed within the 30 minute post-run glycogen window is an effective way to help your body recover after your efforts and also replenish depleted glycogen stores so that you'll be fully energized for your next run. During this window, the enzymes in your body responsible for making glycogen are more active, meaning that glycogen stores can be replenished faster by consuming carbohydrate-rich foods. The plant protein in the vegetables promotes muscle repair and regeneration after a hard effort and also stimulates the action of insulin which boosts glycogen replacement by aiding the transportation of glucose from the blood to the muscles.

Restoring your body's electrolyte balance is an important element of recovery after a long or intense run. Electrolytes are particles that circulate in your blood and help to regulate your body's fluid balance. Long runs can lead to muscle soreness and inflammation but a post-run juice can help to minimize the damage and speed the recovery process.

Fluids and Hydration

Adequate hydration is essential at all times and of particular importance to endurance athletes. Remaining adequately hydrated during a run is essential as fluid in your blood transports glucose to the working muscles and takes away the metabolic by-products. Dehydration has a negative effect on your performance because it causes your blood to thicken, decreases your heart's efficiency and raises your body temperature. Hydration levels can be boosted before a run by drinking a large glass of water and replaced after a run in the same way, but a fresh juice provides a practical way to boost your fluid *and* nutrient intakewithout overloading your stomach and potentially causing discomfort.

Water in Fruits and Vegetables

The water content of the fruits and vegetables you juice can significantly increase your overall fluid intake.

Cucumber - 96 percent water

Lettuce - 96 percent water

Celery - 95 percent water

Zucchini - 95 percent water

Melon - 94 percent water

Red tomatoes - 94 percent water

Cabbage - 93 percent water

Grapefruit - 91 percent water

Watercress - 91 percent water

Strawberries - 89 percent water

Carrots - 87 percent water

Oranges - 86 percent water

Peaches - 86 percent water

Apples - 84 percent water

Grapes - 79 percent water

Juices with a Twist

Combining fruits and vegetables is a delicious way to get the maximum nutritional benefit from a juice. Fruits add sweetness which can make a green juice more palatable, but other great ways to add flavor and interest include:

Ginger - research has found that ginger can be helpful in reducing muscle aches after intense exercise.

Garlic - contains antiviral and antibacterial properties.

Parsley - one cup of parsley contains 2 grams of protein. It is also rich in calcium and provides iron, copper, magnesium, potassium, zinc, phosphorus, beta-carotene and vitamin C.

Dill – adds a sweet flavor to a vegetable juice and contains calcium, iron, manganese, vitamin C, and beta-carotene.

Sorrel - provides iron, magnesium and calcium.

Basil - provides beta-carotene, iron, potassium, copper, manganese and magnesium.

Coriander - provides a mild, peppery flavor along with anti-inflammatory properties, vitamin C, iron and magnesium.

Turmeric - contains antibacterial, antibiotic and anti-inflammatory properties. It also adds a vibrant yellow color!

Nutmeg - adds richness and warmth to any vegetable juice. Works particularly well with cauliflower.

Cayenne - a rich source of vitamin A.

Black pepper - contains iron, beta-carotene, vitamin C and bioflavonoids.

Ginger, garlic and parsley can all be juiced along with fruits and vegetables but dried versions can also be mixed in to "spice up" your juices and add to the nutritional content. Experimentation is the only way to discover the flavor combinations that work best for you. The fresher your ingredients, the more nutritional value they hold, but it is worth noting that frozen produce can represent a good choice when fresh foods may have spent a little longer than ideal on the grocery store shelf. Organic produce will generally offer a healthier choice in terms of the number of chemicals used in the farming process but non-organic produce still provides the nutrients you need to fuel your body and to boost your overall health.

Healthy fat can be added to a juice in the form of extra virgin coconut oil – or any other oil containing essential fatty acids that suits your taste – to provide an extra source of energy-giving calories and anti-inflammatory properties. On-going research into the health benefits of consuming coconuts has found that it may not only help to reduce inflammation, but also support the immune system and promote healthy tissue growth and repair. Of particular benefit to runners is the fact that coconut oil is utilized by the body as a source of energy in preference to being stored as fat and it is now being hailed as the "healthiest oil on earth"!

Getting the Most from a Juice

The more variety and color you have in your diet, the more nutritionally beneficial it's likely to be. Green fruits and vegetables pack a healthy punch but by eating a wider variety of colors and flavors, you optimize your potential to achieve a healthy balance of nutrients. Colorful combinations include:

Beets and carrot

Apple and grape

Carrot and mango

Kale and kiwi fruit

Red cabbage and pear

To gain the maximum nutritional value from your juice, always try to consume it as soon as it's made. The health benefits of fresh produce quickly begin to diminish as soon as it's picked or harvested so local produce is always preferable to produce that has been shipped around the world! Aim to drink a freshly made juice within 24 hours as even when stored in a refrigerator, the absence of preservatives means it will go rancid much faster than a store bought juice.

Other juicing tips include:

Start with fruits that are easily juiced - good choices are oranges and apples. Not all fruits (or vegetables) yield the same amount of juice and if getting a glass-full feels like a lot of effort, you're less likely to repeat the process.

Prepare your ingredients in advance - to make it easier to start your day with a nutritious juice, prepare your fruits and vegetables the night before and store them in an airtight container in your fridge overnight.

Drink your juice at room temperature - a juice at room temperature is easier on your digestive system than a chilled juice. If possible remove your juice or your juicing ingredients from the fridge around 30 minutes before you need them.

Use a variety of fruits and/or vegetables - variety helps to ensure you get a healthful mix of nutrients. It also helps to prevent boredom ... but you don't need to use a mountain of different ingredients in every juice to get the most out of it!

Start simple! - Only a process of trial-and-error will help you to discover the flavor combinations that work and those that don't. However, it's best to stick to no more than three ingredients to begin with and to go for fruits or vegetables you know you normally enjoy. As your juicing experience grows, you may find that combining certain fruits with vegetables you normally avoid is a great way to get your greens without getting their taste!

Using tried-and-tested juice recipes takes the guess work out of creating great flavor combinations but you will soon find your own preferences. Experimenting with different fruits and vegetables is a great way to discover new flavors, and once you get started, you may be surprised by just how many fruits and vegetables there are out there that you never knew existed!

General Information about Your Juices

These smoothies are divided into 3 categories, each designed to meet the nutritional needs of the runner at three specific times:

Pre-run juices ;

Pre-run juices – for high intensity/long runs;

Post-run juices.

The great majority of the ingredients in these recipes have a low Glycemic Index.

If you can't find the fresh fruit you need for a recipe, feel free to replace it with frozen. Frozen fruits have the same nutritional content as the corresponding fresh fruits.

You can adjust the consistency of your juice adding some ice cubes to the recipe before blending and/or straining before serving.

If you are looking for new flavors, try replacing ice the ice cubes in the recipes for frozen cubes of your favorite tea.

Pre-Run Juices

These juices were developed to provide an adequate amount of Carbohydrates to a 150 pounds person. You can adjust the amount of carbohydrates by adding one of the following by each extra 5 pounds of your body weight:

- ½ tsp. of honey;
- 1 tbsp. of flax seed;
- ¼ tbsp. of fruit jam;
- 1 tsp. of seeded raisins;
- ½ tbsp. of dried apricots;
- 3 ½ tbsps. of reduced fat milk;
- 2 ½ tbsps. of low fat yogurt.

1. Strawberry and Mint Juice

Preparation time	5 minutes
Ready time	5 minutes
Serves	1
Serving quantity/unit	550 G 19 Ounces
Calories	275 Cal
Total Fat	2 g
Cholesterol	0 mg
Sodium	13 mg
Total Carbohydrates	69 g
Dietary fibers	10g
Sugars	52 g
Protein	4g

Prepare your juice combining the following ingredients in a juicer/food processor:

- 3 cups of strawberries
- 2 ½ tbsps. of raisins
- 2 tbsps. of fresh mint
- 1 tbsp. of honey
- 3 ice cubes

2. Papaya and Lemon Juice

Preparation time	5 minutes
Ready time	5 minutes
Serves	1
Serving quantity/unit	632 G / 22 Ounces
Calories	266 Cal
Total Fat	1 g
Cholesterol	0 mg
Sodium	18 mg
Total Carbohydrates	69 g
Dietary fibers	10g
Sugars	43 g
Protein	4g

Prepare your juice combining the following ingredients in a juicer/food processor:

- 4 cups of papaya
- ¼ cup of lemon juice
- 1 ½ tsps. of honey

3. Banana, Apple and Cinnamon Juice

Preparation time	5 minutes
Ready time	5 minutes
Serves	1
Serving quantity/unit	500 G / 18 Ounces
Calories	266 Cal
Total Fat	1 g
Cholesterol	0 mg
Sodium	3 mg
Total Carbohydrates	69 g
Dietary fibers	7g
Sugars	41 g
Protein	3 g

Prepare your juice combining the following ingredients in a juicer/food processor:

- 1 ¾ cups of banana
- 1 ½ tsp. of honey
- 1 cup of peach tea

4. Pineapple and Pear Juice

Preparation time	5 minutes
Ready time	5 minutes
Serves	1
Serving quantity/unit	540 G / 19 Ounces
Calories	259 Cal
Total Fat	1 g
Cholesterol	0 mg
Sodium	7 mg
Total Carbohydrates	68 g
Dietary fibers	9g
Sugars	49 g
Protein	2g

Prepare your juice combining the following ingredients in a juicer/food processor:

- 2 cups of Pineapple
- 1 cup of pear
- ½ tsp. of honey
- 3 ice cubes

5. Watermelon, Melon and Pear Juice with Spinach

Preparation time	5 minutes
Ready time	5 minutes
Serves	1
Serving quantity/unit	680 G /24 Ounces
Calories	275 Cal
Total Fat	1 g
Cholesterol	0 mg
Sodium	77 mg
Total Carbohydrates	70 g
Dietary fibers	11g
Sugars	50 g
Protein	5g

Prepare your juice combining the following ingredients in a juicer/food processor:

- 2 cups of spinach
- 1 cup of melon
- 1 ½ cups of watermelon
- 1 ½ cups of pear

6. Kiwi, Pear and Strawberry Juice

Preparation time	5 minutes
Ready time	5 minutes
Serves	1
Serving quantity/unit	520 G / 18 Ounces
Calories	267 Cal
Total Fat	1 g
Cholesterol	0 mg
Sodium	8 mg
Total Carbohydrates	68 g
Dietary fibers	14g
Sugars	43 g
Protein	3g

Prepare your juice combining the following ingredients in a juicer/food processor:

- 3/4 cup of kiwi
- 1 ½ cups of pear
- 1 cup of strawberries

7. Carrot, Orange and Pineapple Juice

Preparation time	5 minutes
Ready time	5 minutes
Serves	1
Serving quantity/unit	600 G /21 Ounces
Calories	289 Cal
Total Fat	1 g
Cholesterol	0 mg
Sodium	83 mg
Total Carbohydrates	69 g
Dietary fibers	4g
Sugars	51 g
Protein	4g

Prepare your juice combining the following ingredients in a juicer/food processor:

- 1 cup of carrot
- 1 cup of orange juice
- 1 cup of pineapple

8. Cucumber, Kiwi and Pear Juice with Mint

Preparation time	5 minutes
Ready time	5 minutes
Serves	1
Serving quantity/unit	532 G / 19 Ounces
Calories	272 Cal
Total Fat	2 g
Cholesterol	0 mg
Sodium	12 mg
Total Carbohydrates	68 g
Dietary fibers	14g
Sugars	41 g
Protein	4g

Prepare your juice combining the following ingredients in a juicer/food processor:

- 1 cup of cucumber
- 1 ½ cups of kiwi
- 1 cup of pear
- 1 tsp. of mint
- Ice cubes

9. Pomegranate and Blueberries Juice

Preparation time	5 minutes
Ready time	5 minutes
Serves	1
Serving quantity/unit	480 G / 17 Ounces
Calories	262 Cal
Total Fat	0g
Cholesterol	0 mg
Sodium	3 mg
Total Carbohydrates	68 g
Dietary fibers	5 g
Sugars	53 g
Protein	3g

Prepare your juice combining the following ingredients in a juicer/food processor:

- 2 medium pomegranates
- ¾ cup of frozen blueberries
- 3 ice cubes

10. Apple and Plums Juice

Preparation time	5 minutes
Ready time	5 minutes
Serves	1
Serving quantity/unit	530 G / 19 Ounces
Calories	268 Cal
Total Fat	1 g
Cholesterol	0 mg
Sodium	1 mg
Total Carbohydrates	68 g
Dietary fibers	8 g
Sugars	58 g
Protein	3 g

Prepare your juice combining the following ingredients in a juicer/food processor:

- 2 ½ cups of plums
- 1 cup of apple
- 1 tsp. of honey

11. Pineapple and Peach Juice

Preparation time	5 minutes
Ready time	5 minutes
Serves	1
Serving quantity/unit	625 G / 22 Ounces
Calories	271 Cal
Total Fat	1 g
Cholesterol	0 mg
Sodium	6 mg
Total Carbohydrates	70 g
Dietary fibers	8 g
Sugars	55 g
Protein	4 g

Prepare your juice combining the following ingredients in a juicer/food processor:

- 2 ½ cups of pineapple
- 1 cup of peach
- ½ tsp. of honey
- 3 ice cubes

12. Romaine Lettuce, Apple and Melon Juice

Preparation time	5 minutes
Ready time	5 minutes
Serves	1
Serving quantity/unit	660 G / 23 Ounces
Calories	265 Cal
Total Fat	1 g
Cholesterol	0 mg
Sodium	57 mg
Total Carbohydrates	67 g
Dietary fibers	12 g
Sugars	54 g
Protein	4g

Prepare your juice combining the following ingredients in a juicer/food processor:

- 1 ¾ cups of melon
- ¾ cup of apple
- 2 cups of romaine lettuce

13. Cucumber and Pomegranate Juice

Preparation time	5 minutes
Ready time	5 minutes
Serves	1
Serving quantity/unit	580 G / 20 Ounces
Calories	270 Cal
Total Fat	0g
Cholesterol	0 mg
Sodium	5 mg
Total Carbohydrates	70 g
Dietary fibers	3 g
Sugars	55 g
Protein	3 g

Prepare your juice combining the following ingredients in a juicer/food processor:

- 1 ¼ cups of cucumber
- 2 ½ medium pomegranate
- 3 ice cubes

Pre-Run Juices - for Runs Lasting 4 or More Hours

Like the previous juices, these are also designed to provide an adequate amount of Carbohydrates to a 150 pounds person. Nothing to worry about if you weigh less than 150 pounds, but if you weight more than this, consider adjusting the amount of carbohydrates by adding one of the following by each extra 5 pounds of your body weight.

- ¾ tsp. of honey;
- 1 ½ tbsps. of flax seed;
- 1 tsp. of fruit jam;
- 1 ½ tsps. of seeded raisins;
- 1 tbsp. of dried apricots;
- 5 tbsps. of reduced fat milk;
- 3 tbsps. of low fat yogurt.

14. Orange and Apricot Juice

Preparation time	5 minutes
Ready time	5 minutes
Serves	1
Serving quantity/unit	600 G /21 Ounces
Calories	415 Cal
Total Fat	1 g
Cholesterol	0 mg
Sodium	15 mg
Total Carbohydrates	102 g
Dietary fibers	7g
Sugars	86 g
Protein	6g

Prepare your juice combining the following ingredients in a juicer/food processor:

- 1 ¾ cups of orange juice
- 2/3 cup of dried apricots
- 3 ice cubes
- ½ tsp. of honey

15. Coconut, and Guava Juice with Lemon and Mint

Preparation time	5 minutes
Ready time	5 minutes
Serves	1
Serving quantity/unit	690 G / 24 Ounces
Calories	582 Cal
Total Fat	19 g
Cholesterol	0 mg
Sodium	21 mg
Total Carbohydrates	103 g
Dietary fibers	35g
Sugars	64g
Protein	16g

Prepare your juice combining the following ingredients in a juicer/food processor:

- ½ cup of coconut
- 3 ½ cups of guava
- ¼ cup of lemon juice
- 1 ½ tsps. of honey
- 1 tsp. of mint

16. Passion Fruit and Raspberries Juice

Preparation time	5 minutes
Ready time	5 minutes
Serves	1
Serving quantity/unit	550 G / 19 Ounces
Calories	435 Cal
Total Fat	4 g
Cholesterol	0 mg
Sodium	85 mg
Total Carbohydrates	104 g
Dietary fibers	47 g
Sugars	50 g
Protein	10 g

Prepare your juice combining the following ingredients in a juicer/food processor:

- 1 ¼ cups of passion fruit
- 2 cups of raspberries
- 1 tsp. of honey

17. Cherry Juice

Preparation time	5 minutes
Ready time	5 minutes
Serves	1
Serving quantity/unit	400 G / 14 Ounces
Calories	434 Cal
Total Fat	1 g
Cholesterol	0 mg
Sodium	17 mg
Total Carbohydrates	104 g
Dietary fibers	25g
Sugars	68 g
Protein	5g

Prepare your juice combining the following ingredients in a juicer/food processor:

- 1 ½ cups of cherries
- ½ cup of dried cherries
- 1 tsp. of cherry jam
- 5 ice cubes

18. Kiwi and Plum Juice

Preparation time	5 minutes
Ready time	5 minutes
Serves	1
Serving quantity/unit	640 G / 23 Ounces
Calories	416 Cal
Total Fat	3 g
Cholesterol	0 mg
Sodium	14 mg
Total Carbohydrates	104 g
Dietary fibers	16 g
Sugars	70 g
Protein	6 g

Prepare your juice combining the following ingredients in a juicer/food processor:

- 2 cups of kiwi
- 1 cup of plum
- 1 tsp. of mint
- ¼ cup of prune
- 1 tsp. of honey
- 3 ice cubes

19. Mango and Pear Juice

Preparation time	5 minutes
Ready time	5 minutes
Serves	1
Serving quantity/unit	650 G /23 Ounces
Calories	386 Cal
Total Fat	1 g
Cholesterol	0 mg
Sodium	11 mg
Total Carbohydrates	102 g
Dietary fibers	13 g
Sugars	81 g
Protein	3 g

Prepare your juice combining the following ingredients in a juicer/food processor:

- 2 cups of mango
- 1 ½ cups of pear
- 1 ½ tsps. of honey
- 3 ice cubes

20. Pineapple, Banana and Broccoli Juice

Preparation time	5 minutes
Ready time	5 minutes
Serves	1
Serving quantity/unit	580 G / 20 Ounces
Calories	412 Cal
Total Fat	2 g
Cholesterol	0 mg
Sodium	37 mg
Total Carbohydrates	105 g
Dietary fibers	13g
Sugars	63 g
Protein	6g

Prepare your juice combining the following ingredients in a juicer/food processor:

- 2 cups of banana
- 1 ¼ cup of pineapple
- ½ cup of brocoli
- 1 tsp. of honey
- 5 ice cubes

21. Melon, Kiwi, Pear and Watercress Juice with Mint

Preparation time	5 minutes
Ready time	5 minutes
Serves	1
Serving quantity/unit	750 G / 26 Ounces
Calories	414 Cal
Total Fat	3 g
Cholesterol	0 mg
Sodium	53 mg
Total Carbohydrates	103 g
Dietary fibers	20g
Sugars	68g
Protein	7g

Prepare your juice combining the following ingredients in a juicer/food processor:

- 1 cup of melon
- 2 cups of kiwi
- 1 ½ cups of pear
- 1 cup of watercress
- 1 tsp. of mint

22. Papaya and Prunes Juice

Preparation time	5 minutes
Ready time	5 minutes
Serves	1
Serving quantity/unit	492 G / 17 Ounces
Calories	395 Cal
Total Fat	1 g
Cholesterol	0 mg
Sodium	14 mg
Total Carbohydrates	103 g
Dietary fibers	14 g
Sugars	62 g
Protein	4 g

Prepare your juice combining the following ingredients in a juicer/food processor:

- 2 ¼ cups of papaya
- 2/3 cup of prunes
- 3 ice cubes

23. Blackberries, Raisins and Beet Juice

Preparation time	5 minutes
Ready time	5 minutes
Serves	1
Serving quantity/unit	530 G / 19 Ounces
Calories	415 Cal
Total Fat	2g
Cholesterol	0mg
Sodium	142mg
Total Carbohydrates	102g
Dietary fibers	21g
Sugars	71g
Protein	9g

Prepare your juice combining the following ingredients in a juicer/food processor:

- 2 cup of blackberries
- ½ cup of raisins
- 1 cup of beetroot
- 4 ice cubes

Post-Run Juices

These juices constitute are richer in protein, providing great combinations of carbohydrate and protein which will be essential to give your body the right nutrients, enhancing its recovery after your ride.

24. Raspberry and Lemon Juice

Preparation time	5 minutes
Ready time	5 minutes
Serves	1
Serving quantity/unit	570 G / 20 Ounces
Calories	282 Cal
Total Fat	3 g
Cholesterol	0 mg
Sodium	7 mg
Total Carbohydrates	68 g
Dietary fibers	28g
Sugars	32 g
Protein	5 g

Prepare your juice combining the following ingredients in a juicer/food processor:

- ½ cup of raspberries
- ¼ cup of lemon juice
- 1 tsp. of honey
- 3 ice cubes

25. Banana and Blackberries Juice

Preparation time	5 minutes
Ready time	5 minutes
Serves	1
Serving quantity/unit	470 G /17 Ounces
Calories	278 Cal
Total Fat	2 g
Cholesterol	0 mg
Sodium	4 mg
Total Carbohydrates	69 g
Dietary fibers	15g
Sugars	36 g
Protein	5g

Prepare your juice combining the following ingredients in a juicer/food processor:

- 1 ½ cups of banana
- 1 ¼ cups of blackberries
- 3 ice cubes

26. Coconut, Papaya, Guava Juice

Preparation time	5 minutes
Ready time	5 minutes
Serves	1
Serving quantity/unit	570 G / 20 Ounces
Calories	419 Cal
Total Fat	16 g
Cholesterol	0 mg
Sodium	21 mg
Total Carbohydrates	69 g
Dietary fibers	22 g
Sugars	41 g
Protein	9 g

Prepare your juice combining the following ingredients in a juicer/food processor:

- 2 cups of papaya
- 1 ½ cup of guava
- ½ cup of coconut
- 3 ice cubes

27. Currants and Lemon Juice

Preparation time	5 minutes
Ready time	5 minutes
Serves	1
Serving quantity/unit	460 G / 16 Ounces
Calories	267 Cal
Total Fat	1 g
Cholesterol	0 mg
Sodium	5 mg
Total Carbohydrates	68 g
Dietary fibers	17 g
Sugars	39 g
Protein	6 g

Prepare your juice combining the following ingredients in a juicer/food processor:

- ½ cup of currants
- ¼ cup of lemon juice
- 1 ½ tsps. of honey

28. Guava and Cherry Juice

Preparation time	5 minutes
Ready time	5 minutes
Serves	1
Serving quantity/unit	530 G / 19 Ounces
Calories	314 Cal
Total Fat	3 g
Cholesterol	0 mg
Sodium	9 mg
Total Carbohydrates	69 g
Dietary fibers	21 g
Sugars	48 g
Protein	10 g

Prepare your juice combining the following ingredients in a juicer/food processor:

- 2 cups of guava
- 1 cup of cherries
- 3 ice cubes

29. Beetroot, Blackberry and Strawberry Juice

Preparation time	5 minutes
Ready time	5 minutes
Serves	1
Serving quantity/unit	700 G / 25 Ounces
Calories	299 Cal
Total Fat	2g
Cholesterol	0mg
Sodium	170 mg
Total Carbohydrates	70g
Dietary fibers	21 g
Sugars	44 g
Protein	8g

Prepare your juice combining the following ingredients in a juicer/food processor:

- 1 ½ cups of blackberries
- 1 ¼ cups of beetroot
- 1 cup of strawberries
- ½ cup of banana
- 3 ice cubes

30. Passion, Fruit and Lemon Juice

Preparation time	5 minutes
Ready time	5 minutes
Serves	1
Serving quantity/unit	370 G / 13 Ounces
Calories	276 Cal
Total Fat	2 g
Cholesterol	0 mg
Sodium	69 mg
Total Carbohydrates	69 g
Dietary fibers	25 g
Sugars	37 g
Protein	6g

Prepare your juice combining the following ingredients in a juicer/food processor:

- 1 cup of passion fruit
- ¼ cup of lemon juice
- 1 ½ tsps. of honey
- 3 ice cubes

31. Cucumber, Watermelon and Cherry Juice

Preparation time	5 minutes
Ready time	5 minutes
Serves	1
Serving quantity/unit	650 G / 23 Ounces
Calories	275 Cal
Total Fat	2 g
Cholesterol	0 mg
Sodium	5 mg
Total Carbohydrates	68 g
Dietary fibers	8 g
Sugars	56 g
Protein	6 g

Prepare your juice combining the following ingredients in a juicer/food processor:

- 1 ¾ cups of watermelon
- 2 cups of cherries
- 1 cup of cucumber

32. Loquat, Peach and Apricot Juice

Preparation time	5 minutes
Ready time	5 minutes
Serves	1
Serving quantity/unit	650 G / 23 Ounces
Calories	277 Cal
Total Fat	2g
Cholesterol	0 mg
Sodium	3 mg
Total Carbohydrates	68 g
Dietary fibers	11 g
Sugars	43 g
Protein	6g

Prepare your juice combining the following ingredients in a juicer/food processor:

- 1 cup of loquat
- 2 cup of peach
- 1 cup of apricot
- ½ cup of strawberry tea

33. Currant and Blackberry Juice

Preparation time	5 minutes
Ready time	5 minutes
Serves	1
Serving quantity/unit	650 G / 23 Ounces
Calories	289 Cal
Total Fat	2g
Cholesterol	0mg
Sodium	8mg
Total Carbohydrates	67 g
Dietary fibers	29 g
Sugars	37 g
Protein	8g

Prepare your juice combining the following ingredients in a juicer/food processor:

- 1 ¼ cup of currant
- 3 cup of blackberries
- ½ tbsp. of blackberry jam
- 3 ice cubes

34. Pumpkin, Orange and Lemon Juice

Preparation time	5 minutes
Ready time	5 minutes
Serves	1
Serving quantity/unit	650 G / 23 Ounces
Calories	262 Cal
Total Fat	1g
Cholesterol	0 mg
Sodium	14 mg
Total Carbohydrates	68 g
Dietary fibers	14 g
Sugars	42 g
Protein	6 g

Prepare your juice combining the following ingredients in a juicer/food processor:

- 1 ½ cups of orange
- 1 cup of pumpkin
- ½ cup of lemon juice
- 1 tsp. of honey

35. Apricot and Guava Juice with Kale

Preparation time	5 minutes
Ready time	5 minutes
Serves	1
Serving quantity/unit	510 G / 18 Ounces
Calories	310 Cal
Total Fat	4g
Cholesterol	0mg
Sodium	36mg
Total Carbohydrates	68g
Dietary fibers	19 g
Sugars	41 g
Protein	11g

Prepare your juice combining the following ingredients in a juicer/food processor:

- 1 cup of apricot
- 1 ½ cups of guava
- ¼ cup of banana
- 1 cup of kale

Exclusive Bonus Download: Sprints And Marathons

> **Exclusive For Readers Only**
> **BONUS REPORT**
> "Sprints And Marathons"
> **GET IT NOW!!**
> Use your PC or Mac to download your bonus report at
> http://simplesportsnutrition.com/runnersjuices

Download your bonus, please visit the download link above from your PC or MAC. To open PDF files, visit http://get.adobe.com/reader/ to download the reader if it's not already installed on your PC or Mac. To open ZIP files, you may need to download WinZip from http://www.winzip.com. This download is for PC or Mac ONLY and might not be downloadable to kindle.

Sure-fire Ways To Master Your Running Efforts!

This Book Is One Of The Most Valuable Resources In The World When It Comes To Getting Serious Results In Your Life!

Running is the act by which animals, including human beings, move by the power of the feet. Speeds may vary and range from jogging to a sprint. A lot of individuals compete in track events that place participants in a contest to test speed in a sprint or endurance in a marathon. The running mechanics are the same, but additional factors are very different in a marathon versus a sprint.

Consider this...

Whether your goal is to determine a fresh personal record in your next 5k, win your age bracket at the following charity run or qualify for a state or national contest, you may learn to run faster.

Are you ready?

Introducing… Sprints And Marathons

This powerful tool will provide you with everything you need to know to be a success and achieve your goal.

Who Can Use This Book?

- Life Coaches
- Runners
- Personal Development Enthusiasts
- Self Improvement Bloggers
- Business owners
- Internet marketers
- Network marketers
- Web Publishers
- Writers and Content Creators
- And Many More!

Visit the URL above to download this guide and start achieving your weight loss and fitness goals NOW

One Last Thing...

Thank you so much for reading my book. I hope you really liked it. As you probably know, many people look at the reviews on Amazon before they decide to purchase a book. If you liked the book, could you please take a minute to leave a review with your feedback? 60 seconds is all I'm asking for, and it would mean the world to me.

******

Books by This Author

The Smoothies for Runners Book

Juices for Runners

Smoothies for Cyclists

Juices for Cyclists

Paleo Diet for Cyclists

Smoothies for Triathletes

Juices for Triathletes

Paleo Diet for Triathletes

Smoothies for Strength

Juices for Strength

Paleo Diet for Strength

Paleo Diet Smoothies for Strength

Smoothies for Golfers

Juices for Golfers

About the Author

Lars Andersen is a sports author, nutritional researcher and fitness enthusiast. In his spare time he participates in competitive running, swimming and cycling events and enjoys hiking with his two border collies.

Lars Andersen

Published by Nordic Standard Publishing

Atlanta, Georgia USA

NORDICSTANDARD PUBLISHING

Lars Andersen

Copyright © 2012 Lars Andersen

Images and Cover by Nordic Standard Publishing

Made in the USA
Lexington, KY
23 March 2014